Aim, Focus, Drive: Mastering the Triad of Workplace Effectiveness

Volume 3:

By Ethen Norton

About the Author

Ethen Norton stands at the forefront of integrating human resource management with technological innovation in the vacation rental sector. As the HR Operations and Technology Manager for VTrips, a frontrunner in the vacation rental industry, Ethen has played a crucial role in embedding advanced technology into HR strategies to boost operational efficiency and spark innovation. His journey reflects a deep-seated passion for technology, beginning from his early education in computer magnet schools in Jacksonville, Florida, and culminating in a significant leadership role that impacts the industry at large.

With a finance degree from Keiser University, Ethen possesses a solid foundation that allows him to navigate the complex relationship between business operations and technology seamlessly. This unique combination of financial expertise and a profound interest in human resources positions him as a strategic thinker, adept at understanding and leveraging the potential of technological advancements to reshape the corporate environment.

Ethen's career trajectory has been anything but conventional. From his early days of exploring computing, he has always been driven by the desire to find practical and impactful applications for technology in the business world. At VTrips, he has gone beyond the traditional confines of HR management by pioneering the integration of AI tools, such as ChatGPT, to streamline operations and solidify the company's reputation as an innovator in the vacation rental market.

Beyond his professional achievements, Ethen is a fervent advocate for technological advancement within his industry. He actively engages with peers, sharing insights and encouraging the adoption of technology to refine business processes. His vision extends beyond immediate operational improvements, aiming to foster a broader understanding of how technology can fundamentally transform business practices for the better.

When not navigating the intersection of HR and technology, Ethen indulges his passion for the latest tech trends, continuously learning and experimenting with new innovations. His story, from a tech-enthusiastic child to a recognized industry authority, is a testament to his relentless dedication, deep expertise, and visionary approach to harnessing technology in revolutionizing the vacation rental industry.

Table of Contents

Introduction: The Journey to Professional Effectiveness 5

Chapter 1: Introduction to the Triad 7

Chapter 2: The Power of Aim 10

Chapter 3: Harnessing Your Focus 13

Chapter 4: Cultivating Your Drive 19

Chapter 5: Integrating Aim, Focus, and Drive for Maximum Effectiveness 23

Chapter 6: Overcoming Obstacles to Aim, Focus, and Drive 27

Chapter 7: Tools and Resources for Enhancing Aim, Focus, and Drive 30

Chapter 8: Advanced Strategies for Balancing and Integrating Aim, Focus, and Drive 34

Conclusion: Navigating the Path to Professional Excellence 38

Introduction:
The Journey to Professional Effectiveness

In today's rapidly evolving professional landscape, the ability to navigate complexities, drive innovation, and achieve personal and organizational goals is more critical than ever. Yet, the path to achieving such levels of effectiveness is fraught with challenges, from the distractions of a hyper-connected world to the internal battles against procrastination and dwindling motivation. This book, "Aim, Focus, Drive: Mastering the Triad of Workplace Effectiveness," is crafted to guide you through the intricate dance of balancing these essential elements to unlock your full potential.

The Essence of Aim, Focus, and Drive

At the core of professional success lie three interdependent elements: aim, focus, and drive. Your *aim* provides a clear direction and purpose, *focus* allows you to channel your energies efficiently, and *drive* fuels your journey towards achieving your goals. Individually, each plays a pivotal role in shaping your professional journey; together, they form a powerful triad capable of propelling you to unprecedented levels of success and fulfillment.

Why This Book?

This book is born out of the recognition that while many professionals possess the skills and knowledge required for success, effectively integrating aim, focus, and drive remains a formidable challenge for many. Through a carefully curated journey, we will explore each element in depth, uncovering insights, strategies, and practical activities designed to enhance your understanding and mastery of these critical components.

Navigating the Book

Structured to build upon each concept progressively, the book starts by delving into the individual elements of aim, focus, and drive, exploring their nuances and providing actionable strategies for development. As we progress, we transition into advanced techniques for integrating these elements, offering a holistic approach to achieving professional effectiveness. Each chapter is crafted to not only provide insights but also engage you in activities that translate theory into practice, ensuring that the knowledge gained is not just understood but lived.

For Whom Is This Book?

Whether you're a seasoned professional seeking to refine your approach to work, a newcomer eager to set a strong foundation for your career, or someone in between, this book offers valuable insights and strategies. It is for anyone who aspires to achieve more, to transform their professional journey into one marked by growth, achievement, and personal fulfillment.

Embarking on Your Journey

As you turn the pages, you're invited to engage deeply with the content, to reflect on your current practices, and to experiment with the strategies provided. This book is not just to be read but to be experienced, serving as a guide and companion on your journey to mastering aim, focus, and drive.

The path to professional effectiveness is both challenging and rewarding. It demands commitment, resilience, and a willingness to grow. But for those who embark on this journey, the rewards are immeasurable. Welcome to "Aim, Focus, Drive: Mastering the Triad of Workplace Effectiveness." Your journey to professional excellence starts now.

Chapter 1: Introduction to the Triad

In the heart of Silicon Valley, a small tech startup faces what seems like an insurmountable challenge: they must launch a revolutionary product in just three months. The task appears daunting, the timeline unrealistic, and the stakes sky-high. Yet, guided by clear aim, unwavering focus, and relentless drive, the team navigates through this tumultuous period. This story isn't unique to the tech world; it's a scenario that plays out in various forms across industries and professions, embodying the critical importance of aim, focus, and drive in achieving success.

The Significance of Aim, Focus, and Drive

Aim is your compass; it's what gives direction to your efforts and decisions. In the context of a career or business, having a clear aim means understanding where you want to go and what you want to achieve. It's the vision that inspires and the goal that guides.

Focus, on the other hand, is the ability to direct your attention and efforts towards your aim, without getting sidetracked by distractions or deterred by setbacks. It's what enables you to dive deep, to master skills, and to complete tasks that move you closer to your goals.

Drive is the inner force that propels you forward. It's a combination of motivation, determination, and resilience. Drive is what keeps you going when the going gets tough, fueling your efforts to overcome obstacles and reach your aim.

The Interconnectedness of Aim, Focus, and Drive

Imagine these three elements as the legs of a tripod: each is crucial to maintaining balance. Without a clear aim, focus and drive have no direction. Without focus, aim and drive are scattered and ineffective. Without drive, aim and focus lack the energy to be realized. Together, they form a powerful triad that can propel individuals and organizations to remarkable achievements.

Here, the essential synergy among aim, focus, and drive becomes evident. Aim without focus is but a dream, focus without drive is fleeting, and drive without aim is directionless. The true power lies in their unity, a harmony that fosters unparalleled growth and achievement.

Why This Matters Now More Than Ever

The workplace today is more dynamic and competitive than ever. Technological advancements are accelerating, industries are being disrupted, and the way we work is fundamentally changing. In this context, the ability to set a clear aim, maintain focus, and sustain drive is more important than ever. It's what distinguishes the successful from the merely busy, the innovators from the followers.

This modern landscape demands not just adaptability and resilience but a clear sense of direction, the capacity for deep work, and the energy to persist in the face of challenges. These are not just skills but essential traits for thriving in an ever-evolving professional environment.

Objectives of the Book

This book is designed to guide you through the process of developing your aim, enhancing your focus, and cultivating your drive. Through a mix of insights, strategies, and real-world examples, you will learn how to navigate the challenges of the modern workplace and achieve your professional goals. Each chapter is dedicated to exploring one of the triad's elements in depth, providing you with the tools you need to integrate them into your professional life.

Call to Action

As you embark on this journey, take a moment to reflect on your current levels of aim, focus, and drive. Consider your long-term goals, your daily distractions, and what motivates you to keep pushing forward. This self-reflection is the first step toward mastering the triad of workplace effectiveness.

Engage with the concepts presented, apply the strategies, and observe the transformation in your professional life. Let this book be a catalyst for your growth, driving you toward unprecedented success.

Key Takeaways

Aim, focus, and drive are interconnected and essential for achieving professional success.

Developing a clear aim provides direction; maintaining focus ensures progress; and cultivating drive overcomes obstacles.

The modern workplace demands proficiency in all three areas for individuals and organizations to thrive.

As we move on to the next chapter, we'll dive deeper into the concept of Aim, laying the groundwork for your journey towards mastering the triad of workplace effectiveness. Prepare to explore how setting a clear aim is not just about defining what you want to achieve but understanding why it matters to you and your organization.

Chapter 2:
The Power of Aim

The journey toward workplace effectiveness begins with a clear aim. Aim serves as the cornerstone upon which focus and drive are built, providing direction and purpose to our professional endeavors. In this chapter, we delve into the essence of aim, exploring its role in shaping our careers and the strategies to define and refine it for maximum impact.

Defining Aim: Vision for the Future

Aim is more than just a set of goals; it's a comprehensive vision for the future. It encompasses our aspirations, values, and the impact we wish to have in our professional sphere and beyond. This vision acts as a guiding star, influencing our decisions, shaping our priorities, and motivating us to move forward even in the face of adversity.

Activity: Envision Your Professional Future. Take a moment to reflect on where you see yourself in five, ten, or fifteen years. Consider the kind of work you're doing, the impact you've made, and the values you're upholding. Write down your vision in as much detail as possible.

Setting Goals: Turning Vision into Action

With a clear aim established, the next step is translating this vision into actionable goals. Effective goal-setting involves breaking down your overarching aim into specific, measurable, achievable, relevant, and time-bound (SMART) objectives. This process transforms your vision from a distant dream into a series of steps you can act upon today.

Activity: Create Your Goal Map. Start with your long-term vision and identify the key milestones you need to achieve to make this vision a reality. Break these milestones down into smaller goals, and set timelines for each. Ensure each goal aligns with the SMART criteria.

Aligning Actions with Aim

The true power of aim lies in its ability to inform and guide our daily actions. Every task we undertake, every project we initiate, and every decision we make should ideally bring us closer to our aim. This alignment ensures that our efforts are focused and our resources are utilized efficiently.

Strategy: Daily Alignment Check. At the start of each day, review your tasks and priorities. Ask yourself how each activity contributes to your broader goals. Adjust your plans as necessary to maintain alignment with your aim.

Navigating Challenges

While a clear aim provides direction, the path to achieving it is seldom straight. You'll encounter obstacles, distractions, and possibly even changes in your own aspirations. Navigating these challenges requires flexibility, resilience, and sometimes, a willingness to recalibrate your goals.

Tips for Navigating Challenges:

Stay Flexible: Be open to adjusting your goals as you gain new insights and experiences.

Build Resilience: Develop strategies to maintain motivation and perseverance in the face of setbacks.

Seek Feedback: Regularly review your progress and seek feedback from mentors or peers. Use this feedback to refine your approach.

Case Studies: Aim in Action

To illustrate the power of aim, let's explore a few case studies of individuals and organizations that have achieved remarkable success by maintaining a clear and compelling aim.

Individual Case Study: A profile of a professional who achieved a significant career transformation by setting and pursuing a bold new aim.

Organizational Case Study: An examination of a company that redirected its business strategy based on a revised aim, leading to unprecedented growth and innovation.

Conclusion: Your Aim is Your Anchor

Your aim is not just a destination but a compass that guides your professional journey. It shapes your focus, fuels your drive, and ultimately determines the impact you make. As you move forward, let your aim be the anchor that keeps you grounded in your values and vision, even as you navigate the complexities of the workplace.

Activity: Reflect and Commit. Revisit the vision you outlined at the beginning of this chapter. Commit to one action you will take this week to move closer to one of your goals. Write it down and place it somewhere you will see it every day.

Next Steps

Having established a clear aim, the next step in mastering workplace effectiveness is harnessing your focus. In the next chapter, we will explore strategies for enhancing focus, minimizing distractions, and maintaining momentum toward your goals.

Chapter 3:
Harnessing Your Focus

With a clear aim setting the direction for our professional journey, focus becomes the vehicle that propels us toward our goals. In this rapidly changing world, where distractions are plentiful and attention spans are tested, the ability to harness focus is more valuable than ever. This chapter delves into the essence of focus, offering strategies to sharpen this vital skill.

Understanding Focus: The Art of Concentration

Focus is the art of directing our attention and energy towards a single task or goal, minimizing distractions and maximizing productivity. It's not just about working hard but working smart, ensuring that each effort brings us closer to our aim.

Activity: Self-Assessment of Focus Levels. Reflect on a recent workday and categorize your activities into focused work, distracted work, and downtime. This will help you understand your current focus patterns and identify areas for improvement.

The Enemies of Focus: Identifying Distractions

In our digital age, distractions are everywhere, from the incessant pings of notifications to the lure of endless scrolling on social media. Identifying these distractions is the first step in mitigating their impact on our focus.

Strategy: Digital Detox. Allocate specific times of the day for checking emails and social media, and use tools or apps that limit your access to distracting websites during work hours.

Building a Focus-Friendly Environment

Our environment plays a crucial role in our ability to focus. A cluttered, noisy, or chaotic workspace can significantly hinder our concentration, while a clean, quiet, and organized environment can enhance it.

Tips for Creating a Focus-Friendly Environment:

Declutter Your Workspace: A tidy workspace can lead to a clear mind. Take time to organize your desk and remove unnecessary items.

Use Noise-Canceling Headphones: If noise is a distraction, consider using noise-canceling headphones to create a bubble of concentration.

Optimize Lighting: Ensure your workspace is well-lit, preferably with natural light, to reduce eye strain and boost alertness.

The Power of Deep Work

Deep work is the ability to focus without distraction on cognitively demanding tasks. It's in these deep work sessions that our most valuable and productive work is done.

Strategy: Schedule Deep Work Sessions. Block off dedicated times in your calendar for deep work sessions, where you can focus on your most challenging and important tasks. During these sessions, minimize interruptions by turning off notifications and informing colleagues of your focus time.

Cultivating a Focus Mindset:

Mindfulness and Focus: Mindfulness practices, such as meditation, can enhance your ability to focus by training your brain to stay present and attentive to the task at hand. Begin or end your day with a short meditation session to cultivate a mindset conducive to focus.

Prioritization is Key: Not all tasks are created equal. Use the Eisenhower Box or a similar prioritization method to distinguish between tasks that are urgent, important, both, or neither. Focus your energy on tasks that are both urgent and important to ensure you're making progress where it counts.

The Pomodoro Technique: This time management method involves working in blocks of time (typically 25 minutes), called "Pomodoros," followed by a 5-minute break. After four Pomodoros, take a longer break. This technique can help maintain high levels of focus and prevent burnout.

Embracing Monotasking

In a world that often glorifies multitasking, the power of monotasking—focusing on one task at a time—cannot be overstated. Multitasking can lead to decreased productivity and increased errors. Embrace monotasking to ensure that your work is of the highest quality and efficiency.

Activity: For one week, commit to monotasking during your deep work sessions. Note any differences in your productivity, the quality of your work, and your overall stress levels.

Overcoming Procrastination

Procrastination is a common barrier to focus. Understanding why you procrastinate—whether due to fear of failure, perfectionism, or simply not knowing where to start—can help you develop strategies to overcome it.

Strategies to Combat Procrastination:

Break Tasks into Smaller Steps: Large projects can feel overwhelming. Break them into smaller, more manageable tasks to avoid feeling paralyzed by the scope of the work.

Set Deadlines for Yourself: Create a sense of urgency by setting your own deadlines, ideally a few days before the actual deadline, to avoid last-minute rushes.

Reward Yourself: Set up a reward system for completing tasks or for productive work sessions to create positive reinforcement.

Maintaining Focus in Long-Term Projects

Staying focused on long-term projects requires a balance of sustained effort and regular rejuvenation. Periodic reviews of your goals and progress can help maintain alignment with your aim and ensure that your focus remains sharp.

Techniques for Sustaining Focus:

Regular Review Sessions: Schedule weekly or monthly review sessions to assess progress, adjust goals as necessary, and plan for the upcoming period.

Stay Flexible: Be open to adjusting your approach based on what is and isn't working. Flexibility can help maintain momentum even when faced with challenges.

Conclusion: Focus as Your Fuel

Your ability to harness focus is a significant determinant of your success in achieving your professional goals. By cultivating a focus-friendly environment, embracing monotasking, overcoming procrastination, and maintaining focus on long-term projects, you equip yourself with the tools to navigate the demands of the modern workplace effectively.

Activity: Implement one focus-enhancing strategy from this chapter in your daily routine. Observe its impact on your productivity and overall satisfaction with your work.

Looking Ahead

With a clear aim defined and strategies for harnessing your focus in place, the next chapter will explore the third pillar of workplace effectiveness: Drive. We will delve into cultivating the inner motivation that propels you toward your goals, ensuring that your aim and focus translate into tangible progress and achievements.

This chapter provides a comprehensive guide to mastering focus in the workplace, offering practical advice, strategies, and activities designed to enhance concentration and productivity. By recognizing the importance of focus and implementing the discussed techniques, you can significantly improve your work efficiency and quality. As we move forward, remember that focus is not just a skill to be developed but a practice to be integrated into every aspect of your professional life.

Reflection and Commitment

As we conclude this chapter on harnessing your focus, take a moment to reflect on the strategies that resonated most with you. Which technique do you believe will make the most significant difference in your daily work life? Commit to trying this technique over the next month, and keep a journal of your progress. Noticing the changes in your productivity and the quality of your work can be incredibly rewarding and motivating.

Preparing for Drive

With a well-defined aim guiding you and enhanced focus propelling your daily efforts, the stage is set to explore the final element of our triad: Drive. Drive is the relentless energy that fuels your journey toward your goals, helping you to overcome obstacles and persist in the face of challenges. In the next chapter, we will uncover the nature of drive, exploring how to cultivate and sustain this powerful force within ourselves. You'll learn strategies for building resilience, staying motivated, and rekindling your drive when it wanes. The integration of aim, focus, and drive forms the foundation of true workplace effectiveness, enabling not only the achievement of your goals but the realization of your full professional potential.

Chapter 4: Cultivating Your Drive

With a clear aim to guide us and refined focus to keep us on track, we now turn our attention to the third and final pillar of our triad: Drive. Drive is the inner fire that propels us forward, the relentless determination to pursue our goals despite obstacles or setbacks. This chapter explores the essence of drive, offering strategies to cultivate, sustain, and harness this vital energy to achieve unparalleled success in the workplace.

Understanding Drive: The Engine of Achievement

Drive is more than just temporary motivation; it's a deep-seated determination that fuels our journey towards our goals. It encompasses our passion, resilience, and the intrinsic motivation that pushes us to excel. Understanding the components of drive—why we strive for certain goals, what motivates us internally, and how we rebound from failures—is crucial for cultivating it effectively.

Activity: Identifying Your Why. Reflect on your professional goals and the aim you've set. Why are these goals important to you? Understanding your "why" is critical for sustaining drive; it's what you'll come back to when faced with challenges.

Building Resilience: The Foundation of Drive

At the heart of drive is resilience—the ability to bounce back from setbacks and continue pushing forward. Resilience is not about avoiding failure but learning from it and using it as a stepping stone towards your goals.

Strategies for Building Resilience:

Embrace Failure as a Learning Opportunity: Instead of viewing failure as a setback, see it as a chance to gain valuable insights and grow.

Develop a Growth Mindset: Believe in your ability to learn and improve. This mindset encourages resilience by framing challenges as opportunities to evolve.

Cultivating Passion: Fueling Your Drive

Passion is the emotional component of drive; it's what excites us about our work and gives us a sense of purpose. However, passion doesn't always come naturally; it often needs to be cultivated and nurtured.

Tips for Cultivating Passion:

Align Work with Interests and Values: Seek projects and roles that resonate with your personal interests and values. This alignment can naturally increase your passion for your work.

Seek Out Challenges: Engaging in challenging but achievable tasks can heighten your interest and investment in your work, fostering passion.

Sustaining Motivation: Keeping the Fire Burning

Maintaining a high level of motivation over the long term is challenging but essential for sustained drive. Motivation can fluctuate, influenced by both internal factors and external circumstances.

Techniques for Sustaining Motivation:

Set Short-Term Goals: Achieving smaller milestones can provide a sense of progress and accomplishment, fueling your motivation to pursue larger goals.

Create a Support Network: Surround yourself with colleagues, mentors, and friends who encourage and support your goals. A strong support network can be a significant source of motivation.

Leveraging Discipline: The Structure of Drive

While passion and motivation are crucial, discipline is the structure that ensures drive translates into action. Discipline is about doing what needs to be done, even when you don't feel like it.

Strategy: Develop Routines and Habits. Establishing daily routines and habits that support your goals can help maintain momentum, even when motivation wanes. Consistent action, fostered by discipline, is key to achieving long-term success.

Conclusion: Drive as Your Compass

Drive, with its components of resilience, passion, motivation, and discipline, acts as the compass that guides you through the challenges and triumphs of your professional journey. It's what pushes you to pursue your aim with unwavering focus, ensuring that obstacles become opportunities for growth rather than reasons for retreat.

Activity: Commit to Action. Choose one strategy from this chapter to implement in your daily routine to strengthen your drive. Whether it's embracing failure as a learning opportunity, aligning your work more closely with your passions, setting smaller goals to sustain motivation, or establishing new routines for discipline, taking action is the first step toward cultivating a stronger drive.

Looking Ahead

As we conclude our exploration of the triad of workplace effectiveness—aim, focus, and drive—we recognize that the journey doesn't end here. The integration and continuous development of these elements are ongoing processes, ones that demand attention and effort. In the next section of our book, we will explore advanced strategies for balancing and integrating aim, focus, and drive into a cohesive strategy for personal and professional growth. Ready to take your effectiveness to the next level? Let's continue the journey together.

Chapter 5:
Integrating Aim, Focus, and Drive for Maximum Effectiveness

With a solid understanding of aim, focus, and drive individually, we now turn our attention to the powerful synergy that arises when these elements are integrated effectively. This chapter delves into strategies for aligning these components to enhance personal and organizational productivity, drive innovation, and achieve long-term success.

The Synergy of Aim, Focus, and Drive

The integration of aim, focus, and drive is not merely about balancing these elements but about creating a dynamic interplay that amplifies their impact. When your aim is clear and compelling, your focus is sharp, and your drive is unwavering, you create an unstoppable force that propels you toward your goals.

Activity: Reflect on Moments of Synergy. Think back to a time when you were highly effective and achieved a significant goal. How did aim, focus, and drive play a role in that success? This reflection can help you understand the power of their integration.

Aligning Your Aim

Alignment begins with your aim. Ensuring that your goals are not only clear but also deeply connected to your values and passions is crucial. This alignment energizes your focus and drive, providing a strong foundation for sustained effort and achievement.

Strategies for Aligning Your Aim:

Revisit and Refine Your Goals: Regularly review your goals to ensure they remain aligned with your evolving interests, values, and the broader organizational objectives.

Visualize Success: Create a vivid mental image of achieving your aim. This visualization can enhance focus and motivation, making your goals feel more tangible and attainable.

Enhancing Focus Through Alignment

With a clear aim in place, enhancing your focus involves creating environments, routines, and practices that support deep work and minimize distractions. Aligning your daily actions with your overarching goals ensures that every effort is meaningful and contributes to your success.

Techniques for Enhancing Focus:

- Prioritize Tasks Based on Goals: Use your aim as a guide to prioritize tasks, focusing on those that directly contribute to your goals.
- Limit Multitasking: Embrace monotasking to enhance the quality and efficiency of your work, allowing for greater progress toward your aim.
- Cultivating Drive with Purpose
- Drive is fueled by a clear purpose and a strong desire to achieve your goals. Cultivating drive involves connecting your day-to-day activities to your larger aim and finding motivation in the progress you're making.

Strategies for Cultivating Drive:

Track and Celebrate Progress: Regularly tracking progress towards your goals and celebrating milestones can boost motivation and reinforce your drive.

Connect Daily Work to Larger Goals: Remind yourself how daily tasks fit into the bigger picture. This connection can make even routine work feel more meaningful and motivating.

Case Studies: Successful Integration

To illustrate the power of integrating aim, focus, and drive, this section explores case studies of individuals and organizations that have achieved remarkable success by effectively aligning these elements.

Individual Success Story: A professional who achieved a significant personal breakthrough by aligning their career goals with their personal values, maintaining rigorous focus, and cultivating relentless drive.

Organizational Achievement: A company that turned around its fortunes by clarifying its strategic aims, fostering a culture of focus, and motivating its employees to drive towards shared goals.

Conclusion: A Unified Approach to Effectiveness

Integrating aim, focus, and drive is not a one-time effort but a continuous process of alignment and realignment. As you grow and your goals evolve, revisiting and refining the integration of these elements will be key to maintaining effectiveness and achieving lasting success.

Activity: Integration Plan. Create a personal plan for integrating aim, focus, and drive in your work. Identify specific actions you will take to align these elements more closely, and commit to regular reviews of your plan to ensure it remains relevant and impactful.

Moving Forward

With a comprehensive understanding of how to integrate aim, focus, and drive, you are now equipped to navigate your professional journey with greater clarity, productivity, and resilience. The next section of our book will explore advanced techniques for maintaining this integration over time, adapting to changes, and continuously enhancing your effectiveness in the ever-evolving workplace landscape.

Chapter 6:
Overcoming Obstacles to Aim, Focus, and Drive

The journey toward integrating aim, focus, and drive is not without its challenges. Obstacles, both internal and external, can disrupt our progress and dampen our effectiveness. This chapter addresses common hurdles to maintaining aim, focus, and drive, offering strategies for overcoming them and staying on track toward achieving your goals.

Identifying Common Pitfalls

Before we can overcome obstacles, we must first identify them. Common challenges include losing sight of our aim, succumbing to distractions, experiencing burnout, and struggling to maintain motivation.

Activity: Personal Obstacle Audit. Reflect on recent weeks and identify moments when your aim, focus, or drive waned. What were the circumstances? Recognizing patterns can help you anticipate and mitigate similar challenges in the future.

Maintaining Aim Amid Change

Changes in our personal lives, careers, or the broader economic landscape can lead us to question or lose sight of our aims. Staying adaptable while maintaining a clear sense of direction is crucial.

Strategies for Maintaining Aim Amid Change:

Flexibility in Your Goals: Allow your aims to evolve as you gain new insights and experiences. Regularly reassess and adjust your goals to ensure they remain relevant and motivating.

Anchor in Core Values: Even as specific goals change, keep your core values constant. They can serve as a steady guide through times of change.

Enhancing Focus in a World Full of Distractions

In today's digital age, distractions are more prevalent than ever. Maintaining focus requires deliberate effort and strategies to shield our attention from the noise.

Techniques for Enhancing Focus:

Digital Hygiene Practices: Implement strict boundaries around technology use, especially social media and email, to protect your focus.

Environment Optimization: Tailor your physical and digital workspaces to minimize distractions. This can include decluttering your desk or using website blockers during work hours.

Sustaining Drive When Motivation Fades

Motivation is not constant; it ebbs and flows. Understanding how to sustain drive even when motivation wanes is key to long-term success.

Strategies for Sustaining Drive:

Reconnect with Your Why: Regularly remind yourself of the reasons behind your goals. A strong emotional connection to your aims can reignite your drive.

Build Resilience Practices: Develop routines that support resilience, such as mindfulness, exercise, and adequate rest, to help you bounce back from setbacks more quickly.

Navigating External Challenges

External challenges, such as organizational changes, economic downturns, or global crises, can significantly impact our ability to maintain aim, focus, and drive. Being proactive and adaptive in the face of these challenges is essential.

Strategies for Navigating External Challenges:

Stay Informed: Keep abreast of changes and potential impacts on your work and goals. Knowledge is power and can help you adapt more quickly.

Seek Support: Leverage your network for advice, support, and opportunities. Collaboration and support can provide new perspectives and resources for overcoming challenges.

Conclusion: Resilience as the Key to Overcoming Obstacles

The ability to overcome obstacles to aim, focus, and drive ultimately comes down to resilience—the capacity to recover quickly from difficulties. By cultivating resilience, you can navigate the inevitable challenges of professional life with grace and continue progressing toward your goals.

Activity: Resilience Action Plan. Identify one area where you frequently encounter obstacles (e.g., losing focus, dwindling motivation) and develop a specific plan to address it. Include strategies for anticipation, immediate response, and long-term adjustment.

Moving Forward

Equipped with strategies to identify and overcome obstacles to aim, focus, and drive, you are better prepared to navigate the complexities of professional growth and achievement. The next chapter will focus on practical tools and resources that can support your journey, offering you additional strategies to enhance your effectiveness and achieve your ambitions.

Chapter 7:
Tools and Resources for Enhancing Aim, Focus, and Drive

Having established a foundation for integrating aim, focus, and drive, and outlined strategies for overcoming obstacles, this chapter introduces practical tools and resources. These aids are designed to enhance your effectiveness in maintaining and capitalizing on the triad of workplace success.

Digital Tools for Goal Setting and Tracking

Effective goal setting and tracking are crucial for maintaining a clear aim. In the digital age, numerous apps and platforms can facilitate this process, offering features like milestone tracking, reminders, and progress reports.

Recommended Tools:

Asana: Ideal for project management and goal tracking, offering visual project timelines and task assignments.

Trello: Utilizes boards and cards to organize tasks and goals, perfect for visual planners.

Evernote: A versatile note-taking app that can be used for goal tracking, journaling, and storing important information.

Activity: Choose a digital tool that resonates with your personal style and integrate it into your daily planning routine. Set up your goals and milestones within the app, and explore its features to enhance your aim.

Focus-Enhancing Software and Apps

Maintaining focus in a world brimming with distractions requires deliberate action. Several apps can help minimize distractions and promote deep work.

Recommended Tools:

Freedom: Blocks distracting websites and apps across all your devices, helping you stay focused on the task at hand.

Forest: Encourages focused work by growing a virtual tree for the duration of your focus session; using your phone before the time is up will kill the tree, promoting digital discipline.

Focus@Will: Provides music and soundscapes scientifically optimized to improve concentration and increase productivity.

Activity: Experiment with one of these focus-enhancing tools during your next deep work session. Note any changes in your productivity and concentration levels.

Motivation and Drive Boosters

Sustaining drive over the long term can be challenging. A combination of digital resources, books, and podcasts can provide continuous inspiration and motivation.

Recommended Resources:

Books:

"Drive: The Surprising Truth About What Motivates Us" by Daniel H. Pink explores the science of motivation.

"Grit: The Power of Passion and Perseverance" by Angela Duckworth discusses the role of grit and determination in achieving success.

Podcasts:

"The Tim Ferriss Show" features interviews with high achievers across various fields, offering insights into their routines and motivation strategies.

"How I Built This" tells the stories of entrepreneurs and the journeys they embarked on to build their companies, offering lessons in persistence and drive.

Activity: Select a book or podcast from the list to explore this month. As you read or listen, identify one strategy or idea to experiment with in your own life to boost your drive.

Creating a Supportive Environment

Beyond digital tools and resources, the environment around you plays a significant role in supporting your aim, focus, and drive. This includes your physical workspace, your social and professional networks, and your approach to health and wellness.

Strategies for Creating a Supportive Environment:

Physical Workspace: Ensure your workspace is organized, comfortable, and conducive to focused work. Consider factors like lighting, ergonomics, and personalization.

Professional Network: Engage with mentors, peers, and professional groups that align with your goals. These connections can offer support, advice, and accountability.

Health and Wellness: Recognize the impact of physical health on mental performance. Regular exercise, adequate rest, and a healthy diet can enhance focus and energy levels.

Conclusion: Equipping Yourself for Success

The tools, resources, and strategies highlighted in this chapter are designed to equip you with everything you need to enhance your aim, focus, and drive. By thoughtfully integrating these aids into your daily routine, you can maximize your effectiveness and move steadily toward achieving your professional goals.

Activity: Develop a Personal Effectiveness Toolkit. Based on the resources and strategies discussed, compile a list of tools and practices you will commit to using regularly. Plan how and when you will incorporate each into your routine for optimal benefit.

Moving Forward

With a comprehensive toolkit at your disposal, the path to achieving and surpassing your professional goals becomes clearer. The final chapter of our book will focus on applying these tools and strategies in a cohesive and strategic manner, ensuring a holistic approach to personal and professional development.

Chapter 8:
Advanced Strategies for Balancing and Integrating Aim, Focus, and Drive

As we approach the culmination of our journey through aim, focus, and drive, it becomes essential to explore advanced strategies for balancing and fully integrating these elements. This final chapter delves into holistic approaches and sophisticated techniques for sustaining and enhancing your professional effectiveness, ensuring that you can navigate the complexities of modern work life with agility and resilience.

The Holistic Integration Model

The Holistic Integration Model proposes a comprehensive approach to intertwining aim, focus, and drive, suggesting that the equilibrium among these elements can evolve as we progress through different stages of our professional journey.

Key Components:

Adaptive Planning: Regularly reassess and adjust your aim in response to new insights, challenges, and opportunities. This dynamic approach ensures that your goals remain relevant and motivating.

Strategic Focus Allocation: Consciously allocate your focus based on the priorities of your current stage, ensuring that you invest your energy where it has the most significant impact.

Drive Renewal Practices: Implement practices that replenish your drive, such as celebrating achievements, engaging in reflective practices, and cultivating gratitude for the journey.

Activity: Reflect on your current professional stage and consider how you might apply the Holistic Integration Model. Identify one area (aim, focus, or drive) needing adjustment and plan a specific action to address it.

Navigating the Aim-Focus-Drive Cycle

Understanding the cyclical nature of aim, focus, and drive can provide valuable insights into managing and enhancing these elements over time. The cycle begins with setting an aim, which then informs where you direct your focus. As you engage in focused action, your drive is both consumed and regenerated by your experiences and achievements.

Strategies for Navigating the Cycle:

- Conduct Regular Reviews: Implement a routine of periodic reviews (monthly or quarterly) to evaluate your progress, reflect on your experiences, and adjust your strategies as needed.
- Mindfulness and Reflection: Use mindfulness practices to maintain a connection with your internal motivations and assess the alignment of your actions with your goals.
- Celebrate Milestones: Recognize and celebrate progress towards your aim, no matter how small, to replenish your drive and reinforce your commitment to your goals.
- Leveraging Feedback Loops
- Feedback loops are mechanisms through which the outcomes of your actions inform and shape your future behavior. Constructively integrating feedback can enhance the effectiveness of your aim, focus, and drive.

Creating Positive Feedback Loops:

Seek Constructive Feedback: Regularly solicit feedback from peers, mentors, and other stakeholders to gain insights into your performance and areas for improvement.

Iterative Learning: Embrace each piece of feedback as a learning opportunity, applying insights gained to refine your approach and strategies.

Self-Evaluation: Develop a practice of self-evaluation to critically assess your progress and adjust your strategies for enhanced effectiveness.

Embracing Flexibility and Resilience

In an ever-changing professional landscape, flexibility and resilience emerge as critical skills for sustaining aim, focus, and drive. Adapting to change, overcoming obstacles, and rebounding from setbacks are essential for long-term success.

Strategies for Building Flexibility and Resilience:

- **Develop a Growth Mindset:** Cultivate a belief in your ability to learn and grow from experiences, which can enhance your resilience and adaptability.
- **Plan for Contingencies:** While remaining committed to your goals, develop contingency plans to address potential challenges, ensuring you can maintain progress even when circumstances change.
- **Practice Self-Compassion:** Recognize that setbacks are a natural part of the growth process. Practicing self-compassion during challenging times can bolster your resilience and drive.
- **Conclusion:** Mastering the Art of Professional Effectiveness
- Mastering aim, focus, and drive is an ongoing process that demands attention, intention, and reflection. By employing the advanced strategies outlined in this chapter, you can ensure that these critical elements are not only balanced but fully integrated into a cohesive framework for sustained professional effectiveness.

Final **Activity:** Develop a Personal Integration Map. Outline a plan that incorporates the advanced strategies discussed, detailing how you will apply these to balance and integrate aim, focus, and drive in your professional life. Commit to revisiting and refining this plan regularly as part of your commitment to continuous growth and development.

Moving Beyond

As we close this book, remember that the journey toward mastering aim, focus, and drive does not end here. The landscape of work and personal growth is ever-evolving, and so too should our strategies for navigating it. Continue to explore, adapt, and grow, and you will find that your capacity for achieving and surpassing your professional goals is limitless.

Conclusion: Navigating the Path to Professional Excellence

As we conclude our exploration into the dynamics of aim, focus, and drive, it's clear that these elements are not just the foundation of professional effectiveness; they are the very essence of personal growth and achievement. Through the chapters of this book, we've journeyed together from understanding each element individually to mastering their integration for maximum impact. This process, though complex, is integral to navigating the multifaceted landscape of modern work life.

The strategies, activities, and insights provided herein are designed to equip you with the tools necessary for cultivating a clear aim, enhancing your focus, and sustaining your drive. However, mastering these elements is not a destination but a continuous process of learning, adapting, and growing. As you move forward, remember that the challenges and obstacles you encounter are not barriers to your success but opportunities for further development and refinement of your skills.

Embrace the Journey

Professional and personal growth is a journey, not a race. Embrace the process, knowing that each step, whether forward or seemingly backward, contributes to your development. Regularly reflect on your progress, celebrate your achievements, and learn from your setbacks. This reflective practice will ensure that your aim remains true, your focus sharp, and your drive strong.

Stay Curious and Open to Learning

The landscape of work and the nature of professional effectiveness are ever-evolving. Stay curious and open to new ideas, strategies, and technologies that can enhance your ability to achieve your goals. Continuous learning is the fuel that will keep your aim, focus, and drive relevant and effective in the face of change.

Cultivate Resilience and Flexibility

Resilience and flexibility are your allies on this journey. They enable you to navigate changes, overcome obstacles, and adapt your strategies as necessary. Cultivate these qualities through mindfulness practices, embracing challenges as learning opportunities, and maintaining a supportive network of colleagues and mentors.

Conclusion

Aim, focus, and drive are more than just concepts; they are the guiding principles for achieving professional excellence and personal fulfillment. As you apply the strategies outlined in this book, you'll find yourself moving closer to realizing your professional aspirations and potential. Remember, the integration of aim, focus, and drive is not just about achieving success in your career but about crafting a meaningful, impactful life.

As we close this book, let it not be the end but a new beginning in your journey toward mastering the art of professional effectiveness. Armed with knowledge, insights, and a comprehensive toolkit, you are well-equipped to navigate the challenges and opportunities ahead. Here's to your continued growth, success, and fulfillment in all your professional endeavors.

www.ingramcontent.com/pod-product-compliance
Lightning Source LLC
Chambersburg PA
CBHW030101230526
45471CB00003B/1205